Social Media

Dominate the Social Media Market and Grow Your Business Worldwide!

Marketing Strategies for Facebook, Twitter, Instagram, and LinkedIn

Table of Contents

This document is geared towards providing exact and reliable information in regards to the topic and issue covered. The publication is sold with the idea that the publisher is not required to render accounting, officially permitted, or otherwise, qualified services. If advice is necessary, legal or professional, a practiced individual in the profession should be ordered.

- From a Declaration of Principles which was accepted and approved equally by a Committee of the American Bar Association and a Committee of Publishers and Associations.

The information provided herein is stated to be truthful and consistent, in that any liability, in terms of inattention or otherwise, by any usage or abuse of any policies, processes, or directions contained within is the solitary and utter responsibility of the recipient reader. Under no circumstances will any legal responsibility or blame be held against the publisher for any reparation, damages, or monetary loss due to the information herein, either directly or indirectly.

Respective authors own all copyrights not held by the publisher.

The information herein is offered for informational purposes solely, and is universal as so. The presentation of the information is without contract or any type of guarantee assurance.

The trademarks that are used are without any consent, and the publication of the trademark is without permission or backing by the trademark owner. All trademarks and brands within this book are for clarifying purposes only and are the owned by the owners themselves, not affiliated with this document.

Introduction

I want to thank you and congratulate you for downloading the book, *"Social Media: Dominate the Social Media Market and Grow Your Business Worldwide! Marketing Strategies for Facebook, Twitter, Instagram, and LinkedIn"*.

This book contains proven steps and strategies on how to use social media for effective marketing and promotions of your business.

We are now living in the social media world, where people are connected with each other through social media platforms. The social media industry itself is a large industry that creates billion-dollar revenue every year.

Aside from its mass appeal, social media has become an integral part of our world today because of its effective and efficient methods in business promotions. It can help start-up companies to establish its customer base, and it could even help companies with their global expansion.

This book will provide you the latest marketing trends and strategies that you can use to market your business to the world through Facebook, Twitter, Instagram, and LinkedIn.

Thanks again for downloading this book, I hope you enjoy it!

Chapter 1 – From Local to Global: Introduce Your Business to the World through Social Media

For most businesses, establishing and sustaining a local customer base is the primary step in achieving entrepreneurial success. Once they have realized this objective, some entrepreneurs think that they are ready to face the next stage: taking the business in the global arena.

Expanding your operations across the world is really a remarkable achievement, and not every business that dreams on doing this will achieve this goal. In order to successfully transform your business from local to global, you need to consider new factors that a local company may not encounter.

Building a strong worldwide presence is seldom as simple as advertising to your customers that you are now providing your products or services worldwide and then just wait customers to contact you. There are many things to consider when you need to sell and market to another country other than the US, and these factors must be carefully integrated in your plans.

Before concerning yourself about social media strategies to dominate the world market, be sure that you answer the following important questions:

Is there an existing customer base in the countries that you want to penetrate?

A product or service that has high demand in your country may not have the same demand in another. Hence, it is important to invest time and effort in knowing more about your prospect foreign markets.

You must first make certain that there is an existing customer base. Is there really a need for your product or service? Are people really willing to buy from you? Never assume that there is a demand for your business. Research. Research. Research.

Visiting the countries that you are interested to expand your business will let you experience a first-hand idea of how your business may perform in the foreign soil. This will provide you the chance to not only perform research and test your products or services, but also to immerse yourself with the social and cultural background of the people that you need to market to.

Is the foreign market you are considering somehow compatible with your current market?

It is ideal to find markets that are similar to your existing market to increase the chance for success. While the business setting will not be totally alike in your home country, you must learn the business environment in your prospect country so you can make the discussions smoother. Consider proximity, trade barriers, culture, and currency. If you are operating in the US, it will be easier for you to conduct business in Canada or UK than in India or Japan.

Do you have the available resources and manpower to work on the expansion and ensure operations of your current business?

Trying to manage worldwide operations while maintaining your local customer base with a limited staff will be extremely hard, and there's a slim chance that you will be able to sustain business growth. Before you expand, be sure that you have the structural and financial stability to add people who can handle the new workload that results from such growth.

If you answer yes to the key questions above, then it is more likely that you are ready for global expansion. And to ensure effective and efficient marketing to your foreign markets, you should consider using social media marketing.

Social Media and Business Global Expansion

Social media is now a crucial channel in business because of its powerful brand-building ability. Still, many businesses are still not reaping the rewards from their investments in social media, because they don't fully understand the core principle in social media marketing: it's not the channel that you use, it's how you use these channels that could provide you brilliant results.

Businesses that have gone global focus their social media activities through careful market segmentation and targeting. While other businesses are floating in the ocean of posts and tweets, smart marketers fine tune and sharpen their social media efforts.

Take a look at these three social media campaigns, which generated huge results through carefully planned targeting.

Little Passports

Little Passports is a company based in San Francisco, which has already built a $5 million business by developing products to offer a global travel experience for kids. As part of its business expansion strategy, the company decided to concentrate its social media efforts through Facebook. They began a comprehensive testing to fine tune their design and message concepts. When they have finally found the right packaging and messaging, they have finally launched a major Facebook ad campaign. In just a span of six months, the company earns $700,000 per month, increased their customer base to almost 300%, and now ships outside the US, specifically to Canada, Denmark, France, Germany, Ireland, Netherlands, Sweden, Australia, New Zealand, Hong Kong, Japan, Singapore, South Korea, and Israel. Its targeted social media campaign helped in laying the groundwork for a successful venture capital infusion of addition $2 million.

Airbnb

Airbnb is a popular online marketplace for people to list and book accommodations across the globe. It was established in 2008 in San Francisco. Today, the company maintains more than 1.5 million listings in more than

34,000 cities around the world. The primary contributor to the company's successful global campaign is through the effective use of social media.

In early 2015, Airbnb started a social media campaign, which was described by the company as a "social, global experiment". Through the campaign, they are encouraging the Airbnb community to perform random acts of kindness by accommodating strangers, and then take photos or videos with the person and sharing it through social media using the hashtag #OneLessStranger.

Unger and Kowitt

The term "glocal" refers to the principle of "Thinking Globally and Acting Locally" But what happens once you reverse this concept?

Unger and Kowitt is a company in Fort Lauderdale that defends drivers who received traffic tickets in Florida. Certainly, this business concept is not global. But the owners of the company understand that Florida is a melting pot of different cultures and social backgrounds.

Even though the company is offering a local service, their website and social media marketing campaigns are available in English, Portuguese, Creole, and Spanish. With these language options, the company caters to more than 3.5 people in Florida who are non-native speakers of English.

There are cases that you don't actually need to look that far to entice global business.

The Challenges of Expanding into a Global Business

While the global market could be an ideal target for your business expansion, there are sure challenges that you will face when it comes to operations, dealings, and marketing. Here are some of them that you must be prepared for.

Cultural and Language

Barriers

Marketing to customers or working with suppliers who don't speak your language can be a large hindrance for your business expansion. Hence, it is crucial to hire personnel who can fluently speak different languages. If you don't want to hire full-time translators, you can outsource the tasks such as translation of social media messages to freelancers.

Aside from language, varying cultural norms could also become an obstacle in a successful global expansion, if you ignore to respect them. It is crucial to learn and understand more about the cultural practices in the countries that you are planning to expand into, as these could play important roles in the development of your social media marketing strategy. Foreign customer needs might not be the same as those in your domestic base, and this may affect not only your social media marketing strategy but also your general business game plan.

Long-winded Steps

In the US, the world of business moves in a fast-paced tempo. From executives to lower-level personnel are willing to work even beyond the work hours to achieve business goals. This is not often the case in other countries. Building relationships with foreign customers may take more time.

Doing business in a foreign country is as much a professional even as it is personal. You can close a sale through formal business meetings or through online channels, but in Asia, it is important to spend time knowing your potential partners during dinner banquets or tea sessions. This is also true in using social media to build trust with your customers. You may need a longer time before you can convert a lead into a customer, but this is not necessarily a bad thing. You need to be patient, and be prepared to launch a long-term social media strategy in order to build trust.

Local Competitors

Similar to traditional marketing, it can be difficult to market to your customers to buy your products, especially if there's a similar product available. You need to work a bit harder to encourage your foreign market that your brand is trustworthy and better compared to your competitors.

Best Practices in Global Business Expansion

If you think you are ready to manage the challenges of global business, consider the following best practices.

Look for the Right Partners

In expanding your business, it's important that you don't do the job alone. You will need help of a person you can trust and who can support your expansion efforts in the country that you are considering to break into.

Find someone who has the same passion for your brand, has enough experience in your industry, understand the local market, and if possible has his own resources to bring on the table, in either industry expertise or financial capital.

Hire the Right People

Find the right people whom you can trust to deal with your partners and customers. They must be completely immersed in the local setting, and you also need to be certain that they are looking out for your business interest. The foreign companies, which you may need to deal with often have more experience doing business in the US than their home country. Without your own team looking for your interests with the significant language, cultural, and local business networks, your global expansion could be in a bad position.

Consider the Effects of New Ideas

Launching a new marketing campaign or introducing new products through social media campaign can become a whole new game, once you go global. Rather than only thinking about the reception of your customers from your home country, you also need to consider the effects of these ideas to your foreign customers.

As you generate new ideas, you

also need to consider about the viability of these ideas to your foreign business. Time differences, language barriers, and cultural appropriateness should be all considered when you expand worldwide.

Be Consistent in Your Branding

As already discussed above, different cultural backgrounds and customer needs in foreign lands may compel you to adjust your social media marketing efforts and even the whole approach in delivering your products. Although you should stay faithful to your branding, it is crucial to customize your products to adapt to the local taste.

Perform Your Due Diligence

Most important business decisions should undergo the careful process of thinking, verifying, and projecting all possible scenarios based on the strengths and weaknesses of your business. This is also true when it comes to global expansion.

Be sure to research every aspect of your business strategy, not only in social media marketing. Find new ways to reach out to your target market and take care of your customer needs. Exhaust every possible way to understand the foreign market you want to break into, and take your time to think things over.

After you are 110% sure that your business is ready for global expansion, it is time to learn proven effective social media marketing strategies that you can use to increase brand awareness, reach out to your target market, and improve engagement among your foreign customers.

Chapter 2 – Global Marketing Strategies for Facebook

In Q1 Facebook statistics for 2015, it is revealed that the number 1 social networking site has more than 1.44 billion active users per month, with 13% increase in users per year.

Facebook also now has 936 million active users every day and 798 million mobile active users every day or 65% of Facebook members are using the site every day. With these numbers, it is fair to say that Facebook is the number one social media platform today, and it should be on your list if you want to market your business worldwide.

Just be sure that Facebook is also widely used in the country or countries that you are planning to expand. There are countries where Facebook is banned or with restrictions such as North Korea, China, Iran, Cuba, Bangladesh, Egypt, Syria, Mauritius, Pakistan, and Vietnam.

That is why you need to hire a team of social media experts who knows the sensitivities of marketing in foreign countries.

In this Chapter, you will learn the most

effective Facebook marketing strategies that can help your business expansion.

Facebook Marketing Strategies for Business Expansion

Leverage the Current Traffic to Your Website

Regardless of the type and nature of your business (whether you are online or offline), it is ideal to run your own website. It will serve as your sales transaction portal or storefront where your existing customers and prospect customers can learn more about your services or buy your products.

You can easily use the current traffic on your website by adding social media icons, which can easily be seen and clicked that are direct links to your Facebook page and other social media accounts.

The best place to put the social media icons is on the header or above the home page, because this is the area where these icons can easily be seen and will lead to higher click-through rates (CTR).

Send E-mail Blasts

Announcing that you are on Facebook is one of the important steps you should do. Email marketing is just one of the ideal ways in order to achieve this. It is recommended to send emails between Monday and Wednesday mornings for higher conversions. Morning emails also result to higher CTR in the US, but you may need to find the general behavior of your target customers if you are marketing in a foreign country. Two of the best tools for email marketing are AWeber and Mail Chimp.

Find the Best Day to Post

One of the most important features that you should learn in Facebook is the Insights. In analyzing your Page Insight, you will see the average time that your fans are online.

If you want to schedule Facebook posts, you can check the best hours that your customers in a certain country are spending time online, and choose those hours to schedule your post.

There are also Social Media tools that you can use such as

SproutSocial and Hootsuite to help you look for the metrics and data you need including the type of post that you must be using for your Facebook posts.

Use Facebook Plugins to Your Website or Blog

Adding Facebook Plugins on your website or blog will improve your branding and increase your followers. For those with sidebars, you can use the Facebook Like Button or Like Box.

For your web pages and blog posts, it's best to add the Like

Button. Still, you can do experiments on what's the best plug-in for your website or blog.

Hold Facebook Contests

Based on a 2013 report, 35% of Facebook users are liking a page so they can join online contests. Customers, regardless of their home country, love freebies and contests. Holding a Facebook contest for your fans will lead to improved page activity and higher engagement. A mere photo-captioning contest can lead to five times more likes compared to regular posts.

If you are selling products, you can give one of your products or other inexpensive stuff as prizes. While if you are providing services, maybe a one-hour consultation or any limited-time offer of your service can be used as prizes. Be certain that your target customers overseas can also join and be sure to promote the contest across all marketing platforms.

Create a Dedicated Facebook Page for Your Geo-Targeted Customers

Once you have started your

operations outside the US, you can choose to create a special Facebook Page for your target customers in specific geographical locations. This will allow you to easily share special promotions that are only intended for customers in that area.

For instance, if you have recently launched your business in Spain and you want to increase Facebook likes, launching a contest for your Spanish customers on your Spanish Facebook page will provide more focus and attention to your marketing efforts.

Engage with Your Facebook Followers

Engaging and conversing with your Facebook followers can forge a strong relationship, loyalty, and trust. The best thing about this is that you can turn these followers into loyal customers. You can also use Facebook as a platform for providing customer service support.

Customize the Images and Videos for Your Content Updates

People are more willing to watch videos or see interesting pictures than to read lengthy text. Images and videos also stand out in Facebook News Feed.

But be sure to customize these images and videos to reflect the language and culture of your customers. For example, North American customers are more attracted to ads using blue and green, while customers in South Asia (India, Pakistan, Bangladesh, etc.) are more attracted to red and orange.

Invest in Facebook Ads

You may not like it, but investing on Facebook ads will help your business to reach your target market. Advertisements on Facebook are not really that costly, and they are worth it once you see the conversion that could boost business expansion. Experiments with different Facebook ads and targeting are important to maximize your marketing efforts.

Take note that Facebook is fast-evolving social media platform. Hence, what is true and effective today might not be effective tomorrow. That is why it is highly recommended to hire Facebook marketing specialists who are consistently updated with the latest trends in Facebook and other social media platforms.

Chapter 3 – Global Marketing Strategies for Twitter

In case you still don't know, Twitter is a microblogging tool, which allows you to send tweets (messages) of up to 140 characters only to people who follow you.

You can use Twitter to share links to any web content such as your own website page, a blog post, a picture, a PDF file, or a video. Adding interesting pictures to your tweets can significantly improve what you can share.

People can follow your Twitter account,

and at the same time your business account can also follow them, which will allow you to engage with them in a more personal level.

Success on Twitter marketing is beyond a series of particular tactics. Rather, this is related to strategic thinking on how you can use this platform for your global online marketing and social media efforts. In this Chapter, we will explore some of the strategies on how you can do that.

Add Your Twitter Efforts with Your Global Content Marketing

Superficially, this strategy might be

oversimplified. For instance, you may easily think that you must share all your key content through your social media channels. Although you can do this, it is important not to overly promote your business.

Integrating your Twitter efforts with your global marketing efforts will call for a different type of mindset.

If you have properly segmented your audience, you should find out what types of shareable content resonate to these audiences such as news, quotes, jokes, etc. Once you fine tune the message according to your global customers, it will drive your content creation and sharing plan.

You can also use Twitter to connect with a wider community such as establishing linkages to global influencers, participating in important conversations, and gaining broader exposure in your industry.

Build Your Worldwide Brand through Twitter

One of the most important objectives in social media marketing is building your brand. You can use Twitter for this end by giving you the vital opportunity to participate in a wider social conversation concerning your niche. Your strategies require you to concentrate on building your brand, so you must take a closer look on every aspect of your engagement on Twitter as a brand-building platform.

Allow Your CEO to Join the Community

Social media is an effective way to engage with your market and establish linkages with your leads, customers, bloggers, and other important connections. But for the Big Boss, the usual channels to social media could be difficult. This is especially true if you are expanding globally. Your CEO usually has minimal time to approve friend requests or reply to messages on Facebook or to write a blog post. But with Twitter's limit of 140 characters, it will be easier for the Top Guy to join the conversation. If your CEO can send a text message to one person, surely he or she can use Twitter to send one message to thousands and even millions of your followers. Twitter is the ideal platform for the business executives who are always on tight schedule but still has the best opinions on your market.

Engage Your Audience through Twitter

Audience engagement is a good way to measure success on social media than the mere number of followers. Take note of how much of your content is being read and shared through Twitter. This is not an entirely new idea for social media marketing, but it is becoming an important factor. The engagement level that organically happens and that you encourage is a good indicator to determine if your Twitter strategy is effective.

Take a closer look at the traffic percentage that Twitter is providing, and the metrics on how often your Twitter links are being clicked. Divert all your efforts to increase this number, as it is a good sign that your Twitter strategy is more aligned with your general funnel plan.

Comments and retweets are a great way to figure out how effective your content is affecting your audience. The more readers are willing to share your material, the more focused your message is with your audience.

Live Updates on Events

Setting up a separate Twitter account for a branch in a foreign country is important when you need to send live updates on local events. For example, if you are participating in a local trade show in UK, you can use Twitter to promote the event or update your followers on what is happening. Your UK customers are highly interested to receive live updates than your customers in the US.

Twitter only allows 140 characters per tweet, so you need to send your message across in that limit. Therefore, you should always have a Twitter specialist in your team who knows how to manage through the technical details of this social networking platform without compromising the quality of the message and the creativity of the whole social media marketing campaign for Twitter.

Chapter 4 – Global Marketing Strategies for Instagram

Instagram is an online mobile application that allows you to capture pictures and videos and share them immediately on social media platforms such as Facebook, Twitter, Flickr, and Tumblr.

The company was acquired in 2012 by Facebook, which has boosted its business growth with 30 billion photos shared, an average 70 million photos posted every day from 300 million active users around the world.

People are using Instagram beyond compare. Based on a research conducted by Forrester, Instagram users are 400% more likely to interact with brands than on Twitter or Facebook, resulting to 58 times more engagement for every follower than Facebook and 120 times more engagement for every follower compared to Twitter.

Hence, Instagram is also an effective channel to build your global brand, and best of all, you can use this platform to more effectively engage with followers to boost sales.

Here are five effective strategies on how

you can get started in using Instagram for your business.

Include Hashtags in Your Promotions

Hashtags are not only essential for Facebook and Twitter promotions. They are also effective in reaching your leads and customers who are on Instagram. You can organize your photos and videos using the appropriate hashtags that could help these media content to appear in live feeds that your prospects are following. Through hashtags, you can drive traffic to your Instagram account, where you can use the profile link to bring traffic back to your website.

Add Your Contacts from Other Social Media Platforms

One way to create your Instagram following and boosting engagement includes identifying customers who are already using Instagram. You just need to export a list of all your customers including their contact details from your CRM or database. Import this list into your Gmail account, and impost the phone numbers and contact details from Gmail into your smartphone, and sign in to your Instagram profile using that phone. Then, use the app's follow all contacts option that will look for any of your contacts on Instagram to easily follow them all. Following 1000 customers is more effective than following 10,000 strangers.

Connect With Influencers

Marketing your business worldwide through influencers is one key in global expansion. Take a look at the case of SHREDZ, a US company that is now distributing nutritional supplements to more than 100 countries around the world. In 2012, they only made about $90,000, but after establishing a partnership with Paige Hathaway, a fitness model, the SHREDZ brand monumentally increased resulting to more than $5 million in gross revenue in 2013. Before the partnership, Hathaway only had 8,000 followers, but now she has more than 1.8 million after three years.

Find influencers in your industry and ask them to be your partners in promoting your products and services. Of course if you are marketing in a foreign country, you may need to find local influencers to encourage more followers and engagements.

Add Instagram Content to

Your Email Marketing

Instagram can be a powerful tool in boosting your email marketing efforts. If you add live Instagram content through brand hashtags, it will be easier for you to simplify the process by providing pictures taken by your customers to leads who are still making the decision to buy your product or avail of your service. This makes your product more appealing and your email marketing more engaging.

Instagram is one of the best tools to develop engagement in your global marketing campaign. Using the power of hashtags, influencers, and other factors, it will be easy for your business to turn Instagram into a strong funnel for generating leads and increasing the quality of customer engagement.

Chapter 5 – Global Marketing Strategies for LinkedIn

If you need to promote a B2B company, it is important that you develop your presence on LinkedIn, which is considered as the most "professional" among the social media platforms. More than 135 business professionals around the world are using LinkedIn. Because it is significantly concentrated on B2B connections, LinkedIn must be a part of your social media marketing strategy for global expansion.

Chances are, you are using LinkedIn as a digital form of your resume. In order to take LinkedIn to the next level and use it to market your business, consider the following strategies.

Improve Your LinkedIn Account

Consider your LinkedIn account as your interactive business profile. With recent updates, you can now use LinkedIn to showcase your business expertise through status updates, blog posts, and presentations.

Status Updates

Among the recommended ways to keep your connections on the loop is by posting status updates, which are short statements that you think can be useful for your connection. You can also add links to related content from your website or other websites. To stay active in the LinkedIn community, it is essential to regularly post actionable and useful status updates. Take note that your status updates must reflect your professionalism, far away from the personal aspects of your life which you can do on Facebook or Twitter.

Blog Posts

LinkedIn allows you to easily integrate your blog posts to your profile. As you add posts to your business blog, your LinkedIn account will immediately update with you're the title, abstract, and link to your post.

Presentations

When you post presentations to Google Docs or SlideShare, you can also display them on your LinkedIn account.

LinkedIn company pages are also optimized for search engines. Google will usually preview up 10 156 characters from your page text, so be sure to edit your company description. Also, members can search for companies through keywords on LinkedIn, so be sure to add words and phrases that are relevant for your business.

Connect with Your Audience

With LinkedIn business pages, you can now easily like and share content as a business. In the previous versions of this channel, you can only do these actions as an individual. This is a major update, which can help you to engage members.

For instance, your page admins can like and reply on comments posted by members as a response to something that you have posted as a business page. Also take time to share the content from your customers or prospects, usually from their product updates, blogs, and business posts in order to drive the conversation. You can also share content from their employees to start building trust with buyers while you are also creating your identity as a professional business brand.

LinkedIn can be an effective tool in global marketing thanks to its targeted updates. You can simply customize your message to your customers. Once you create an update, you may choose to share it with all your followers or a specific set of audience only. You can choose the latter option to send your updates based on geographical location of your customers.

Entice More Followers

Like other social media platforms, it is best to attract more followers in LinkedIn. Here are three strategies you can do to entice more followers with your business updates:

Build a Larger Following with a Multi-Platform Approach

Make sure that everyone in your company adds a link to your LinkedIn page in their email signatures. If necessary, you can ask your graphic designer to help in creating a personalized button or banner.

Connect with Your Audiences

According to research, employees are 70% more likely to engage with your business page updates, so encourage them to achieve this. Start communication and make it easier for them to reply.

Embed a Follow Button to Your Website

Your web developer team can add

code for a LinkedIn follow button to be added to your website or blog. This will allow members to follow your company with only a click.

LinkedIn is considered as the "chamber of commerce" in the social media world. Using this platform to market and promote your business will not only establish business contacts and generate sales, you can also find the best people for your social media marketing team.

Conclusion

Thank you again for downloading this book!

I hope this book was able to help you to leverage the power of social media for the global expansion of your business.

The next step is to make sure that you find the right people who will drive your social media efforts in a cost-effective approach.

Finally, if you enjoyed this book, then I'd like to ask you for a favor, would you be kind enough to leave a review for this book on Amazon? It'd be greatly appreciated!

Thank you and good luck!